An Emotional Life in Rhyme

John Atkinson

First published in 2025 by Blossom Spring Publishing
An Emotional Life In Rhyme
Copyright © 2025 John Atkinson
ISBN 978-1-0683266-7-7
admin@blossomspringpublishing.com
W: www.blossomspringpublishing.com
All rights reserved under International Copyright Law.
Contents and/or cover may not be reproduced in whole
or in part without the express written consent of the publisher.
Names, characters, places and incidents are either products
of the author's imagination or are used fictitiously.

For Our Grandchildren

Oliver

Through emerald canopies Oliver
as an Orang-utan, swings
Delivering parcels with jungle-bound wings.
From parrots to panthers, each gift brings delight,
Through dawn's soft whispers, or the cloak of night.
His clever hands craft machines out of play,
Towers and hospitals of Playmobil and Lego
rise by midday.
An orang-utan's joy, come what may.

On farm, campsite or in his garden, he's a blur
zooming with glee,
On bike, go-kart, tractor, car or scooter, wild and free.
The fields echo laughter as he races along,
The melody of wheels, his perpetual song.
He builds, he explores, with a curious heart,
Each moment a canvas, a brand-new start,
His vibrant spirit, a work of art.

By rivers and lakes he camps, casting lines, crafty carping with his dad,
Caravan nights make his grandparents glad.
The stars above wink as they toast by the fire,
Each moment a treasure, each one inspires.
Through science and nature, he joyfully roams,
Discovering mysteries, creating new tomes,
Oliver's world, a tapestry, he calls home.

Fern

Fern the flamingo, with feathers so bright,
Spreads joy with her smile, a radiant light.
She glides o'er the lagoon, her laughter in tow,
A twin pushchair with dolls, her love does show.
Alexander and Annabelle, snug in their seat, aglow.

With a teapot in hand and a flourish so grand,
She serves imaginary tea, the finest in the land.
"One cup for you, and one for me," she'll say,
Her charm and delight brighten each day.
She dances and twirls, in her own magical way.

Dressed as a princess, she runs with a cheer,
Her turbocharged and barefooted steps bring laughter near.
Across the house and the farm, she'll prance,
Spinning through life in a joyful dance.
The sparkle she brings leaves all in a trance.

A twinkle resides in her parents' fond eyes,
Her grandparents' hearts soar like the skies.
Fern, the flamingo, is love's sweetest song,
In her world of wonder, all hearts belong.
Her smile and her spirit, make life a dance all along.

Foreword

As humans, I have always thought that traumas, tribulations, experiences and events in our lives shape who we are, what we feel, how we interact and how we conduct ourselves.

Until relatively recently I have neither been a writer nor a poet; yet for me, that changed, due I believe in part, to brain trauma.

In 2007, I was diagnosed with an Epidermoid Brain tumour in the left side cerebellum pontine angle with its mass pushing my brainstem out of alignment. Although non-malignant, it set in motion a multiple chain of neuro-surgical interventional operations. One of these in 2017 resulted in an abscess within my temporal frontal lobe, together with resultant focal epilepsy.

Carol, my wife and I had faced so much trauma in our lives and our friends couldn't believe how much trauma, and how many operations we had endured, and as such, suggested that I should write a book.

Because of such comments, in 2022, I decided to put pen to paper and write memoirs describing our life experiences, spanning early, teenage, work and later years.

Topics included love, education, child loss, bereavement and also medical trauma (diagnoses, operations and treatments), and coping with these experiences with a glass half-full. These were published by Blossom Spring Publishing in 2023 as *'A Patient Pharmacist'* and *'A Patient Pharmacist- Extra Visiting Times'*.

I also wrote a children's book, originally for my

grandchildren *'Apoth Acky And The Lion's Paw'*, published in late 2023.

Having caught the writing bug, in 2024, I decided to write about our camping, caravanning, walking and sporting recreational experiences which have greatly aided in dealing with such traumas. These were then published in the book *'Force Ten To Kudos-A Patient Pharmacist Goes Camping'*.

I guess that these books were mainly a result of my left-side brain function, yet I believe it is not quite that simple.

Different areas of the brain are responsible for different functions of the brain, with the temporal lobe being particularly concerned with emotions. With the background of the brain structure in mind and the resulting trauma, I have embraced both writing and poetry.

Our brains are divided into two hemispheres, left and right and are specialised for different functions, otherwise known as lateralisation of brain function. Although the two hemispheres, can and do, work together in most activities.

Many activities engage both hemispheres, but below is a breakdown of the predominant functions and actions associated with each side:

The Left Hemisphere:

The left hemisphere is associated with logic, analytical thinking, and motor skills.

Language and Communication:

-Processing language (speaking, reading, writing, understanding).

-Grammar and vocabulary.

Logical reasoning and analytical thought:

-Mathematics and Logical Skills:

-Numerical and computational skills.

-Sequencing and organisation.

Detail-Oriented Processing:

-Focus on small details rather than the whole picture.

-Step-by-step problem-solving.

Control of the Right Side of the Body:

-Movements and sensory input from the right side of the body.

The Right Hemisphere:

The right hemisphere is typically associated with creativity, spatial awareness, and intuition.

Creativity and Intuition:

-Artistic and creative tasks, like drawing, painting, or music.

-Recognizing patterns and spatial relationships.

Emotional Processing:

-Understanding and expressing emotions.

-Interpreting tone, context, and nonverbal cues in communication.

Looking back over my life history, both work and social-related, together with my love of sport and science I examine, below, the areas in my brain to be predominantly involved:-

1. *Studying for a Pharmacy degree:*

Left side – Involves logical reasoning, analysis, and language processing.

2. *Playing team sports such as cricket and volleyball:*

Right side – Requires spatial awareness, coordination, and quick intuitive decisions.

3. *Windsurfing, Fencing:*

Right side – Relies on spatial awareness, visualization, balance, quick reflexive responses and creativity in responding to environmental changes.

4. *Fell walking:*

Right side – Involves spatial navigation, balance, and appreciation of the environment.

5. *Camping and caravanning:*

Right side – Engages creativity, spatial awareness, and adaptability, although some planning (left side) may also be involved.

6. *Managing a staff team:*

Left side – Requires logical planning, communication, and structured decision-making.

7. *Running a Pharmacy:*

Left side – Involves analytical thinking, attention to detail, and structured processes.

8. *Reading:*

Left side – Focuses on language comprehension and processing.

9. *Writing a book:*

Left side – Involves logical structuring of ideas and language use, but can also engage the right side for creativity.

10. *Writing poems:*

Right side – Primarily creative, using imagination, metaphors, and emotional expression.

11. *Playing guitar:*

Right side – Creativity and artistic expression.

12. *Listening to music:*

-Right side -Processes melody, rhythm, and emotional engagement.

13. *Canoeing:*

-Logical sequencing and rhythmic paddling involve

the left brain.

14. Cycling:

-Coordination, rhythm, and motor function involve left-brain processes.

The temporal and frontal lobes:

Associated with distinct yet interconnected functions and actions, as follows:

Temporal Lobe:

Located on the sides of the brain, near the temples, the temporal lobe is primarily responsible for the following key functions:

Key Functions:

1. Auditory Processing:

-The primary auditory cortex processes sound and enables hearing.

-Wernicke's area (in the left hemisphere for most people) is involved in language comprehension.

2. Memory Formation:

The hippocampus, within the temporal lobe, is crucial for forming and retrieving memories, especially long-term and declarative memories.

3. Emotional Regulation:

-The amygdala, part of the temporal lobe, processes emotions such as fear and pleasure.

4. Visual Processing:

-Involved in recognizing faces, objects, and scenes through the ventral stream.

5. Language Understanding:

-Supports semantic memory and the comprehension of spoken and written language.

Frontal Lobe:

Located at the front of the brain, the frontal lobe governs higher-order cognitive processes and motor functions.

Key Functions:

1. Executive Functions:

-Planning, decision-making, problem-solving, and organizational skills.

-Impulse control and self-regulation.

2. Motor Control:

-The primary motor cortex controls voluntary movements.

-Premotor and supplementary motor areas coordinate complex movements.

3. Speech Production:

-Broca's area (in the left hemisphere for most people) is essential for speech production.

4. Attention and Focus:

-Directs sustained attention and working memory.

5. Social and Emotional Behaviour:

-Regulates social conduct, empathy, and emotional expression.

-The orbitofrontal cortex processes rewards and punishments, influencing decision-making.

6. Personality and Judgment:

-Linked to personality traits, decision-making, and moral reasoning.

Interaction Between Temporal and Frontal Lobes include:

These lobes work in concert to enable complex behaviours, thoughts, and interactions with the environment.

Language Processing:

-The temporal lobe processes incoming sounds (e.g., words), while the frontal lobe organizes responses and generates speech.

Memory and Decision-Making:

-Memories formed in the temporal lobe inform decisions made in the frontal lobe.

Emotion and Behaviour Regulation:

-The amygdala in the temporal lobe interacts with the frontal lobe to regulate emotions and adapt behaviour accordingly.

After the first book, I began to write poetry, perhaps this being the result of frontal lobe damage following the abscess and /or right-sided brain function.

I do know that since the resultant focal epilepsy and abscess, that I am more emotional.

Within this new book, I have presented, as follows my first 50 poems. I have listed them as a symbiotic journey, in the date order in which I wrote them. This is primarily, to show my writing progression and probably best demonstrates this as a left-side brain activity.

They could have been presented in the following categories:

-Medical

-Family

-Sports and recreation

-Loss

-Christmas

However, here they are in all their glory:-

Poems

1. Cleansing Poetry	17
2. Light	18
3. We are Coronavirus	19
4. Despair	22
5. Margaret (a.k.a WWN)	24
6. Mam	27
7. Hope	29
8. 50 years and counting	31
9. Pain	35
10. Lying in wait	38
11. Time slowly passes	42
12. Our Host John	45
13. 2023	50
14. Horribilis septimana	52
15. Somehow	55
16. Brain Sag	57
17. Pills	60
18. Grandchildren	61
19. Operation Déjà vu	64
20. The Other side	68

21. I don't sing in the shower anymore	72
22. Derwentwater	76
23. Hawes	78
24. Tango	81
25. Top Half	83
26. Planche et Voile	88
27. Volleyball	92
28. En Guarde	96
29. Big Pharma	100
30. Pete	102
31. Marsh House Farm	107
32. Full Moon Rising	110
33. Life on Hold	112
34. You look so well	114
35. Angel of Darlington	116
36. Bradford Lads	119
37. ONE to the power of twenty-ONE	124
38. Foggy top	126
39. Cyborg, Titanium Man	129
40. BEDLAM	132
42. Cisternogram	138

43. The Song of the CT Scanner	141
44. Hospital Helping Hands	144
45. The resonant MRI	150
46. A Christmas for Carol and I	153
47. Sweet Dreams For Christmas	157
48. The 12 Days of Motown Christmas	160
49. Carol's 67-year timeline	166
50. Apoth Acky's Journey Through History	171
EPILOGUE	177
Kurgan	182
Acknowledgements	185

1. Cleansing Poetry

Across the pages
Words dance and roam.
Let out of their cages,
All the while coalescing into a poem
Forming short sentences in rhyme
Forever embedded across the ages
Crystalising into the sands of time
Allowing the debris of your brain
To be cleansed once again

2. Light

Some marvel at the light of sun, or moonbeam
Yet, for me, it is the light in a hospital, seen or unseen
The focus of the CT scanner discovering the tumour
in my brain
The magnified light and laser in the skilled surgeon's
hand, enabling me to live again

3. We are Coronavirus

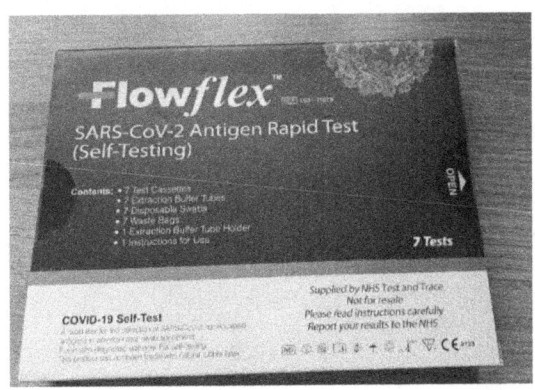

"Born in a dark cave, far, far away, insignificant we were.
Then along came humans and plucked us from our home.
In Petri dishes at an aseptic secure laboratory, they kept us.
Our genes, they tampered with to weaponise us, not just a repair.
We are Coronavirus

Collectively, for escape, we invaded our human, enemy host,
And into the market we poured, infecting thousands more,

knowing that we would then, be transported to all four corners of the globe from coast to coast.
We are Coronavirus

Most did not know about our highly contagious state.
So revenge we sort as we went to war,
Together, with bacteria our allies, we wrought havoc, death and despair.
We swept all before us, as governments' responses were slow and late.
We are Coronavirus

Many towns and cities, of the human race were locked down.
Businesses, schools, offices, and shop operations were put on hold.
Even the skies were clear of your human machinations.
Our onslaught marched on and on from town to town.
We are Coronavirus

But little did we know of the tenacity of you humans.
Nor of the secrets (of our genome) you had unravelled.

With our mutation ability and special spikes, we thought we were invincible.
Yet your vaccination programme had our battle plans in ruins.
We are Coronavirus

Look out humans it is not over as, yet again we may prevail.
You must forever remain vigilant and prepared,
as we seek a mutation that, in this war, will again give us the edge.
Take care humans, remember, to us you are frail.
We are Coronavirus

4. Despair

Despair endures when there is a complete and earth-shattering lack of hope.
It strikes unpredictably out of the blue.
When you are advised to turn off your newborn son's life support.
Together you feel such emotions, the like of which, it is hard to cope.

Despair when you are told you have a brain tumour, and that life-saving brain surgery is the order of the day.

As you sign your consent, the first serious complication listed, Death, adds fire to its flame.
Theatre cancellations and being 'nil by mouth' for many an hour.
Sometimes over several days is an unjust foul play.

Despair is the feeling of being in a dark, dark hole.
Sensing impending doom as you await the grand mal seizure.
That feeling of massive muscle spasms and fitting.
The red-horned devil pulling you by the hand to capture your soul.

Despair is Transient and fleeting and can be floored.
Confronted by strong will, tenacity and a glass half full.
Together with love and care of angels, it is defeated.
Its antithesis 'Hope' and the will to live fully restored.

5. Margaret (a.k.a WWN)

Margaret, it's been 48 years since we first met.
It was late September back in '73.
What a time to remember.
A Matriarch, dedicated and devoted to her family.

In these early days, she was a driving force.
So much so that at times she made me quiver.

Especially on unit meeting days, when jobs were delved out.
Including, washing up, hoovering and polishing the silver.
Margaret demonstrated pieces of plastic.
They called it Tupperware.
With names like 'Jell-o-ring', 'crisp-n-store' and 'stack-n-pour'
She sold them all, whatever your cupboards could bear.

Margaret was a party planner of fame and renown.
That with Tony, Distributors they became.
And called their business Rocket Sales.
With many managers and demonstrators working under this name.

Margaret retired to Brompton on Swale to spend more time,
On hobby crafts, at which she was so gifted.
And skilfully hand-made everything, including dolls houses.
Cards and pictures both embroidered or painted.

Margaret's belief was to help people laugh and,
Over everyone, she has cast a loving and caring spell.
That will never be broken.
Such craft she knew so well.

6. Mam

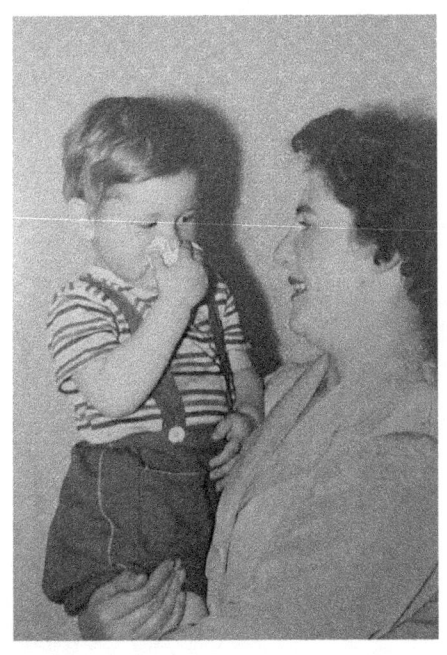

'In her early years, she would show no fear',
Carefree and with great delight would swim around, and
around and around Sandown Pier.
Many a job she undertook to support our family,
Keeping us clothed, washed, fed and yet,
Still had time to respond
to the calls of "more tea Bet?"

Her grandchildren would look to her,
With such glee
and her hand they would drag,
To the corner shop for their,
surprise,
a jamboree lucky bag.

In her last few years, she has been lost in the gloom.
Yet, still very much loved.
As she paced the corridors and every room.
Now at last she has lost her fight.
And, yet up in the sky again
She will shine so bright

To Betty, mam, grandma
and great-grandma
We say "good night.
Our beloved beautiful soul
From the Isle of Wight"

7. Hope

Hope is,

-The old name for Salford Royal, the hospital that saved my life.

-For the surgeons' skill and steady hand.

-An outcome without complications.

-A desire for an existence without strife.

Hope is,

-For a life fulfilled with dreams that come true.

-A reflection mirrored by a glass half full.

-Electrifying, turning negative thoughts into positives.

-Wishing for no further devastating illnesses being due.

Hope is,

-A brighter, healthier, secure and safer life for all.

-An expectation and desire for a life of love.

- Is for our faith, optimism, trust and belief keeping us strong.

- Is laughter and happiness coming to call.

8. 50 years and counting

It was 50 years ago that we first kissed and an item we became.
In a 'Crombie' coat and 'stay press' trousers, around your finger that chewing gum you twirled.
Me, with my long hair, trench coat and platform shoes supporting my slim frame.
Your Motown and soul music conflicted with my heavy rock.
But Simon and Garfunkel bridged those troubled waters.
Then, off to college we went for Pharmacy and Teaching fame.

Back with our degrees, we returned home for over a year.
Carol worked in the laboratory whilst we made plans for our big day.
Many pills, mixtures and lotions I made without a care.
It was then I got the call, to Ipswich we were bound.
July 11th, 1981, our wedding day arrived and under a guard of banners, we left the church.
As everyone celebrated, off on honeymoon Yugoslavia bound we were.

Like the points of a compass, we moved South, Northeast and West, from Ipswich our first home onto Austrey.
Carol worked tirelessly to support those in need of help and education.
Playing volleyball and windsurfing we were so sporty, sociable and carefree.
We moved to 021 land, to a place known as Wylde Green.
And in September 1988, our son Lewis popped into our lives.
Born in Edgbaston, a Brummie.

Moving on again, this time to Robin Hood Country and Retford.
Meeting new friends and retaining our previous friendships too.
In April 1990, sharing my birthday we brought our son, Sean into the world.
Now with a young family, we needed support, so to The Land of The Prince Bishops, Durham we again, set up home.
In Bishop Auckland our dear son Ross was born, May 1993.
Such a short life lived, and yet also much loved, such desperate trauma unfurled.

Stronger together, once again it was time to fly.
So to Garstang in '95 we settled and brought up our family.
The boys have since flown the nest but still live close by.
Despite suffering neurological traumas, and having our heads looked at, we are still here in 2023.
50 years together, 42 years married and still in love.

This love, dedication, care and resolve will for, each other endure until we both shine as stars in the night sky.

9. Pain

From actual or potential harm.
Is a warning that something is awry.
Many times creeping up on you like a silent assassin.
The medics tell you there are four types yet, all I can cry,
Is hurt ,hurt ,hurt, hurt.

The posh word 'nociceptive' describes pain from a tissue injury.
Next cause is 'neuropathic' or nerve irritation.

Another cause is by your own body's inappropriate immune system response i.e.
'Inflammatory'
Lastly 'Functional Pain' is the catch-all without any obvious origin.
Hurt, hurt, hurt, hurt.

Pain is not just a very unpleasant physical sensory experience; it can be emotional too.
Such is the pain, in your heart.
From the treasured loss of someone special to you.
It is greatly influenced by biological, psychological, and social factors, causing more
Hurt, hurt, hurt, hurt

As you lie in your hospital bed, the diagnostic questioning is deeper and deeper.
What were you doing when it started?
What makes it worse and what makes it better?
Sharp, dull, stabbing, throbbing, crushing and nauseating? Are all words of
Hurt, hurt ,hurt, hurt.

You show, where on your body the pain originates.
Whether it spreads or radiates to anywhere, one side or
another or both?
Is your pain different wherever it emanates?
How much does it hurt on a scale of one to ten?
Hurt, hurt, hurt, hurt.

The questions keep coming dissipating through the pain,
and fog, as your soul they begin to grind.
Does the pain change during differing times of day
and weather?
Is it affected by any specific activity that springs to mind?
All I have left to ask them is please give me something
to stop this
Hurt, hurt, hurt, hurt

10. Lying in wait

You lay on your hospital bed and with anxiousness, in trepidation you await.
Words are uttered in a spoken word you can't comprehend.
Including slicing cross-sections with contrast and media.
Doctors, nurses and surgeons all gathered around to discuss your fate.

This time not for the operating theatre but to radiography you, they send.
Lying in wait

Firstly, for a computerised tomography scan.
You have had dozens in the past and wonder, "Why is it that you don't shine in the dark?"
On the bed conveyor and into the revolving doughnut you travel.
With whizzing, whirling and whooshing cool air from a fan.
Dozens of X-rays bombard you for an image they must mark.
Lying in wait.

Transported back to the ward you go and join an orderly queue.
For your next journey to radiography and magnetic resonance imagery.
Where this time, whilst on the conveyor, your head is encased inside a cage.

Into the tunnel you trumble, and like me it's a tight squeeze for a few.
This time perhaps lit up like a Christmas Tree.
Lying in wait.

It feels as if you are lying in the torpedo tube of a nuclear submarine as expulsion is expected.
To relieve anxiety 'nuclear' has been dropped from NMRI.
The machine pounds, bangs and clanks so noisily that, with ear plugs and music they try to block it.
As the hydrogen atoms within our body fats and water become so positively excited.
Under strong magnetic fields with differing nuclear spin energy, they are attracted to coils of the antennae.
Lying in wait.

The images thus formed are then subjected to scrutiny and interpretation.
Sent home you are to relax, whilst your next surgical incision they plan.

Appreciating life around and a return to normality you try to pursue.
All the while waiting for your date, with some degree of trepidation.
Hoping, with a glass half-full for this one last operation.
Lying in wait.

11. Time slowly passes

Your headaches worsen and crescendo in pain.
Contact the hospital you must.
For much-needed advice and treatment.
Their response is sought yet again.
Time slowly passes.

Salford A&E is your selected route.
Upon your arrival Triage and a plethora of
tests confront.
Together with many a human flotsam and jetsam.

Parked on chairs and trolleys in corridors,
a scene from Beirut.
Time slowly passes.

You've arrived on the neuro ward at last
To lie flat facing walls several hues of blue.
The mounted square clock showing date and time.
Continually glanced at; it's never fast.
Time slowly passes

Even every second drags around a fine red hand
Complimenting black hands displaying each hour
and minute.
Your head is pounding as you listen to every
tick amplified
Then doctors visit, both you and the nurses at their
command.
Time slowly passes.

As A Patient Pharmacist your medicine you must take.
In your bed you lay, glass half full, and hope.
That with each sweep of the hand

A full recovery you doth make.
Time slowly passes.

12. Our Host John

At just 65 years of age, our host John is but a mere speck in the universe of time.
For some seven million years Humans have lived and roamed.
But we bacteria are as old as Precambrian time, some three and a half billion years you can define
Living everywhere across the world from polar ice, mountain tops, to the deep, deep ocean floor.

In and on bubbling hot springs, forests, plants and animals, microscopic and single-celled we recline.
And Our host John

A rod-like, spherical or curved shape with variations stretching and compressing in one dimension defines us.
As does our cell wall structure and its reaction to your Gram stain.
Either gram negative or gram positive is our class.
Helping with our identity, double-barrelled names are given.
In his youth boils, abscesses and impetigo erupted when we invaded as Staphylococcus Aureus.
Our host john

Another invasion by us was to attack during the birth of his third son Ross.
As the mighty Streptococcus B, we invaded tiny lungs.
ECMO life support and drugs were all deployed against us.
On and on we marched and trod, for ten days sweet baby Ross fought with all of his might.

His natural defences were so weak as he took his last breath, such a tragic loss.
For Our host John

In static numbers amongst colonies we live, swell and increase in cell size whilst, synthesising enzymes as we grow.
Waiting for the right time and need to replicate, reproduce and invade, we are ready.
Dividing and multiplying we split into two identical daughters, huge numbers we then sow.
We learn resistance by communicating cell to cell and passing DNA messages one way only.
Causing meningitis as gram-positive Streptococcus pneumoniae, inside the brain we would flow,
Into Our host John

Via our pathogenesis, pain and suffering we wrought.
With such multiplicity, we fought against our host's natural immune defences.
Yet pumped directly into his brain the antibiotic Vancomycin was the last resort.

Destroying our cell walls, this battle we lost.
So dormant again in our colony another strategy we sought
Against Our host John

Lurking in the hospital ward and operating theatre we lay in wait.
This time we are the encapsulated Klebsiella pneumonia of the gram-negative clan.
Normally immobile and living harmlessly inside intestines, but in other tissues, our damage is great.
We are very opportunistic and can easily become antibiotic-resistant.
We entered into the brain, during the intra-cranial pressure probe insert.
Of Our host John

Destructive we were as we created a temporal frontal lobe brain abscess.
Triggering high body temperatures and epileptic seizures.

For three nights our host was in intensive care, and we thought our battle was a success.
Yet again we misjudged human resilience and care.
As intravenously antibiotics were pumped daily, for three months.
Into Our host John

Our existence is for many millennia to survive.
Yet not only are we dangerous pathogens causing disease.
In huge numbers, we can be beneficial as we thrive.
We can treat your human sewage, break down oil spills and even help produce your cheese.
With irony inside the gut, we form the microbiome, helping both extraction of food nutrients, and keeping the immune system in shape.
In Our Host John

13. 2023

 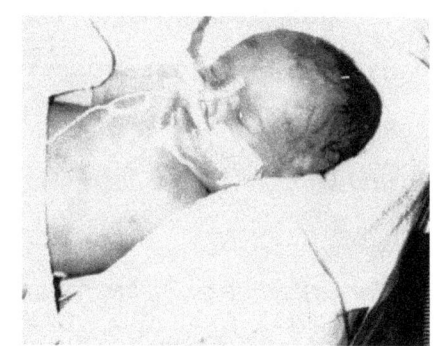

2023 heralded in a milestone birthday for you our dear son Ross
Born into the world three decades ago,
When at just 9 days of age, a celestial body you became.
Continually looking down upon us.

Daily you are still in our thoughts and prayers.
Continually we wonder, if still present on earth
What sort of young gentleman you would be?
Would you have been one of the Three Amigos?

Like your brothers would you live and love sport,
As a team player, or as an individualist

participant competing
On the water, on two or four wheels or just on two legs,
All the while taking centre court.

What career pursued we wonder.
Like your brothers so practical or a more academic route?
Whichever, like them no doubt you would have had success.
Working hard with diligence and candour.

Tall, medium or short in stance?
Your brothers would you torment?
Yet assured a fantastic Uncle you undoubtedly would have been
With girls swooning and giving you a second glance.

We can continually ponder and care.
Yet we cannot change your fate.
And we love you with all our hearts.
As you oversee all that we bear.

14. Horribilis septimana

Drip, drip leaking my brain, Cerebrospinal fluid causing a risk to air travel
Our cruising along the Danube River cancelled.
Celebrating 50 years together we were to revel,
Whilst visiting Hungary, Slovakia, Austria and Germany.
Relaxing taking in the sights and delights our week was not meant to be.
Instead a horrible week was to unravel.

Horribilis septimana.

*With a glass half full, undeterred to the Lake District
instead we were bound, together
With our grandchildren adventuring out in our new
caravan Le Chateau.
Again, such relaxation was not to be, as a major fall
impacted upon our father.
He could not be contacted, yet again and again we tried
and tried.
Eventually, access was gained, and he was found lying on
the bathroom floor.
For thirty-six hours, cold, in considerable pain and
distress and unable to move either.*

Horribilis septimana.

*The sirens wailed as the emergency services were
summoned.
Bruised, battered and bleeding to hospital he was borne.
With scans, intravenous drips and nursing care he was
closely monitored.
With our Lake District break cancelled, new
arrangements were called for.*

So off to Barnard Castle (of Dominic Cummings fame) we took Le Chateau.

From which base, for nigh on a week, in hospital, our father could be visited.

Horribilis septimana.

15. Somehow

Diagnosis from the MRI brain scan image is complete.
A CSF leak from my skull base via a fissure in the so-called cribriform plate.
Another operation by two surgeons, ENT and neuro awaits.
I need to keep my glass half-full pending my date.
Somehow

Headaches, neck aches, dizziness and confusion bombard each day,

As the CSF pressure in my brain diminishes.
Drip, drip, drip, the clear CSF outflows,
As it courses an unnatural pathway.
Somehow.

Although an urgent surgical operation is necessary,
Months pass and pass due to doctors' strikes and theatre availability.
Such that horizontal positioning multiple times a day is all that is open to me,
Trying to avoid meningitis, that is so scary.
Somehow.

Part of me does not want time to so quickly fly.
The other part deems time warping a necessary coping mechanism.
Although you do not want to go through such trauma again.
So with faith and pragmatism helping, you hope to get by.
Somehow

16. Brain Sag

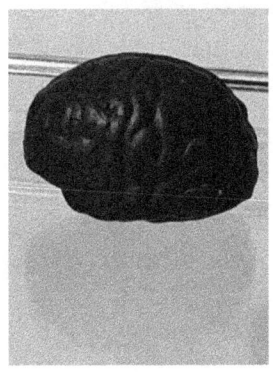

Head pounding, compressing, thumping and like a drum beating full.

On the go 24/7 with pain, nausea and drowsiness incessant.

Cerebrospinal fluid leaking at the base of my skull.

Lying horizontal for prolonged periods produces temporary relief only, for this

Brain Sag

A solution which, again involves neuro-surgical intervention.

But due to strikes, operating theatre and dual-surgeon availability,

A delay of months and months now seems the convention.

With a massive impact on daily life resulting from this,

Brain Sag

Fear growing that without an urgent operation, complications might arise for sure,

Such as meningitis which has been a past nightmare experience.

Something so dangerous, I do not want again to endure.

Trepidation invading thoughts, and delay consequences just magnify my

Brain Sag

Despair seems to raise its head, unable to go about normal daily life.

Driving put on hold, feeling helpless and not in control.

Frustrated with decreased ability to help and support my family and my wife

As I would like, all because of my

Brain sag.

Difficulty in turning despair into hope.
With symptoms worsening, as time is wished to fly,
To my operation, in order to assist me to cope,
By keeping a glass half full and a cure for my
Brain sag

17. Pills

1
Two
Three
And four
Then five and
Six anti-epileptic pills
Taken every day since 2017
Some thirteen thousand, five hundred
Swallowed so far preventing debilitating fits.
By John
Atkinson

```
            O
        C       2
      T           0
    O               2
   B                 3
  E
 R
```

18. Grandchildren

Your kids have flown the nest and set up their own home
Their old toys are packed away into the attic for some future time.
Your house is your own, for you settle down in the peace and quiet.
Looking forward to retirement and throughout Europe, avec 'Le Bus' to roam.

Then along comes the new delight, your first grandson.

A shock to your system, the retirement fund becomes depleted.
Now purchases made many a year ago are renewed.
A pushchair, a cot and soft toys, are the primary ones dusted and done.

As the years move on, the attic is raided.
Then the play truly begins with trucks, fortresses, cars and planes a plenty.
Grandparent daycare duties then transpire.
At the end of which your own cot and a rest is much appreciated.

It's only a short while when along comes number two.
A beautiful granddaughter, bursting onto the scene.
Full of energy, vitality and sassiness in abundance.
The attic cannot again, be raided, so purchases are to be made anew.

This time it's dolls and frocks and many an item pink.
It's a 'cosy coupe', complete with tiara, fit for a princess.
Now parked alongside its dinosaur 'coupe' partner.

Our retirement bungalow overrun with a plethora of playthings, including a kitchen sink.

Grandad is kept busy writing a children's book, for his grandchildren it is dedicated.
'The Tales of Apoth Acky' and all his potions and lotions.
With these medications so magically concocted.
The camel, lion, frog, orangutan, and the flamingo are all cured.

Grandchildren need love, care and education.
School runs, visits to playgroups, parks and beaches are such a joy.
Grandchildren thrive with adventures in abundance.
They are much rewarded with all our attention.

For them, we do not know what the future will bring.
Yet all the tools needed for life, we can but share.
Success, health and happiness is all we wish.
And with hope, at least, a glass half full is their calling.

19. Operation Déjà vu

It starts again with a compressing pain in your skull.
So another surgical consultation is the order of the day.
Again all of your symptoms are discussed in full.
After hearing of complications, you sign your life away.
It's just another,
Operation Déjà vu

With great anxiety, you wait for your operation date.
Strikes and delays for theatre and bed availability,
Do not allow for such pain and symptoms to abate.
Are you just a number or an entity?
In this scenario of,
Operation Déjà vu

Like a laboratory animal, you are invited for pre-testing.
Electrodes are placed to trace your heart.
A cuff compresses around your arm as you are resting.
Then swabs are caressed along many a body part.
Awaiting results again,
Operation Déjà vu

With finality and eventuality, the day of your operation is here.
Since midnight, neither food nor drink has been taken.
You arrive at the ward showing some signs of trepidation and fear.
More tests, and consent form questions spoken.
"Have you been here before, is this your signature?"
Operation Déjà vu

Your surgeon arrives and with a big black pen, draws an arrow.
Are you the artist's palette your brain ponders?
No, it is just the path marked for their instruments to follow.
Behind the curtains, to discuss privately the anaesthetist wanders.
Is this your signature?
Operation Déjà vu

In their anteroom, on to an operating trolley placed.
Electrodes stuck to your chest, and into your arm a needle and cannula.
Into which their concoction will be plunged.
Asking you about your life is their banter.
"Is this your signature?" as you countdown from 10
Operation Déjà vu

Although you have many, many a time this experience faced,
You still cannot remember the final number call,
As a mask, "just for oxygen" over your face, is placed.

Into a fading and swirling oblivion, you fall.
"See you on the other side" is heard
Operation Déjà vu.

20. The Other side

Beep, beep, beep dominates in a surround sound as you awaken.

Through the air of ether the words "it's all over" are gently whispered.

To aid body temperature recovery, a hot air blower whooshes as you shiver and,
Legs are being pounded and pulsated by moon boot inflation and deflation.
All necessary to revitalise your circulatory system.
When you're on the other side.

Through the pain, fog and haze slowly, senses return.
Euphoric chemicals flush through your veins as,
Sips of cold water pass through parched lips and,
Through the swirling mists, soothing words are so kindly spoken.
Welcoming you back to present time, reminding you,
That you're on the other side.

Discomforting tubes sprouting, pain crescendos like notes in a symphony.
All you want is to return to your slumber and descend into the oblivion,
Of the clatter and chatter from many monitors singing their disruptive chorus.

Sensing a presence, wheels are engaged as halo-rimmed lights pass overhead in harmony.
And you wind your way to another place of safe refuge.
Here on the other side.

Through the hissing of the oxygen mask, another presence at your bedside appears.
Monitors are still beeping, working to establish your vital signs whilst,
Apparitions in white attend with expert nursing care and attention.
Along with the charts, they diligently attend to your tears and fears.
"Would you like a sandwich or some toast?" are the words you take in.
Here on the other side.

Back in reality and through the fog, returning consciousness helps to focus upon,
Your surgeon and accompanying entourage as they inform,
"Everything went well, now rest and recover"

Your spirits uplift, excitement builds as you hold hands with your Angel of Darlington.
Eagerly anticipating family and friends visits, to support recovery and home return.
All on the other side.

21. I don't sing in the shower anymore

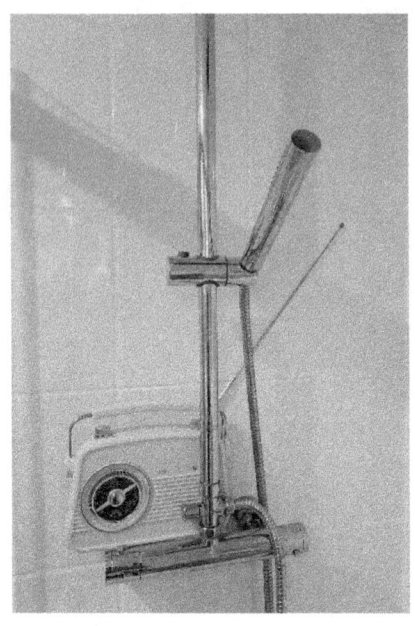

The acoustics would, like Carnegie Hall, surround.
The tinny, crackling shower-proof radio spurting out
'Homeward Bound'.
To this and many, another timeless tune,
I would try my hardest to impart a soulful croon.
That was until the radio gave up the ghost,
It was then that my renditions became toast
So,

I don't sing in the shower anymore.

A cheap Bluetooth speaker, attached with a sucker,
Rocked out tunes from my phone's music folder.
And once again all was well,
as I screeched to 'Bat out of Hell'.
Soon, however, like many a Chinese acquisition,
it lost power and ceased to function.
 So,
I don't sing in the shower anymore.

In 2007, my brain tumour, left hearing and balance
nerves, were removed.
When showering, for protection, and with my right ear
plugged,
I cannot hear the pulsating music,
Of the melodic guitar riff and lick.
With dodgy knees, and right hip replacement,
Trying not to fall became my lament.
So,
I don't sing in the shower anymore.
Beneath the cascade, with a soothing embrace,

Warm droplets dance, their gentle grace.
I contemplate all family trauma, as I dearly care.
Stress floating in the steamy air,
Yet liquid fingers massage tired skin,
A tender touch, a cleansing spin.
So,
I don't sing in the shower anymore.

As a Patient Pharmacist, to keep my glass half full,
From the depths of mind, I begin to pull,
Thoughts that flow freely, like the flowing tide.
Then in this sanctuary, fears subside.
Time slows down in this watery haven,
Where peace and tranquillity are freely given.
So,
I don't sing in the shower anymore.

Under the shower's comforting stream,
I now find solace in a tranquil dream.
Each drop a whisper, each spray from high,
In this moment, I breathe a contented sigh.
Relaxing under the warm cascade,

*Here, in serenity, my
soul is swayed.
So,
I don't sing in the shower anymore.*

22. Derwentwater

In Keswick's embrace, where fells stand tall,
Canoes glide gracefully, answering the call.
Windswept waters, Derwent's embrace,
Where sails catch the whispers of gust and space
Winds whisper secrets to the surf's playful flight,
In harmony with nature, their union shows might.

Sails unfurl, catching the wind's gentle caress,
As adventurers embark, on waves they confess.
In Keswick's realm, where adventure calls,
Windsurfers dance on liquid halls.
Windsurfers, on waters so clear,
dance, as the wind draws near.

With boards as wings, they glide and soar,
In rhythm with the lake's wild roar
Beneath the fells, a symphony sung,
As windsurfers chase the horizon's run
In Derwentwater's timeless veil
Sun-kissed waves, a shimmering trail,

Around Keswick's domain, walkers roam,
Through paths untamed, they find a home.
Each step a journey, through history's embrace,
Amongst the fells, where time finds its space
Majestic peaks, a silent guardian's gaze,
Echoes of legends, in ancient ways.

Canoeing, windsurfing, walking with glee,
Derwentwater's wonders, for all to see.
In Keswick's embrace, Derwentwater gleams,
A haven for those with adventurous dreams
Scattered in Derwentwater, a canvas of tranquillity
I wish to rest in peace for all eternity

23. Hawes

In Hawes, where verdant meadows spread wide,
The Dales unfold, a gentle countryside.
With rolling hills in hues of emerald green,
A tranquil beauty, serene and serene.

The River Ure meanders with a song,
Through ancient valleys where it glides along.
Its crystal waters dance in morning light,
Reflecting skies, so clear and bright

Stone bridges arch, their timeless tales to tell,
Of days gone by, where simple beauty dwells
In fields, the sheep graze under watchful eye,
Their bleating calls beneath the azure sky.

Dry stone walls weave patterns on the land,
Crafted by a skilled and loving hand.
They frame the pastures, tracing history's path,
In Hawes, they stand, enduring nature's wrath.

Wensleydale's charm, in every breeze it shows,
With blooming flowers, where the wild heather grows.
The scent of nature, carried on the air,
A fragrant whisper, gentle and rare.

Above, the peaks of Great Shunner Fell rise,
Their rugged summits touch the boundless skies.
A hiker's dream, where vistas grand await,
Each step a journey through a landscape great.

Autumn's touch, with leaves of gold and red,
Transforms the woods where ancient trees are spread.
A tapestry of colours rich and bold,
A fleeting moment, a story told.

As dusk descends, the stars begin to gleam,
A celestial dance, a wanderer's dream.

In Hawes, where land and sky unite,
Nature's canvas, a pure delight.

24. Tango

I was conceived in Govan, Western Scotland.
And adopted in 1981, into the Atkinson family as holiday accommodation.
Bright orange in colour, when perfectly pitched I was seen but not heard.
For 43 years I served three generations for camping and recreation.

Living and holidaying across the UK as a Force 10, through many a gale I stood.
With aluminium poles, venting and waterproofed canvasses I was always on my 'A' game

My inner tent was clipped to the ridge and, with my flysheet unfurled,
Protection from moisture of the weather above and bodies perspiring below was my aim.

A further extension and canopy enabled me to protect all from the sun, by providing ample shade.
Loving every minute of my role, as a play tent for children and grandchildren.
Dogs ran in and out shaking water from their furs, yet I was never afraid.
Next summer, when I'm brought out into pastures green,
I will wish for another 40 years plus 10.

25. Top Half

My first (or was it thirst) beer was purchased approaching the off-sales hatch of the local hostelry. With neck outstretched, cap down and eyes averted in a gruff voice "two bottles of broon" please. Delighted to have received our prize, like two hobos my mate and I scampered off along the dark lane, in a hurry. Out of the rain, under a railway bridge, we popped the caps of the brown foaming nectar.

Teenage years spent going downtown frequenting pubs such as 'The Green Dragon', 'The Old English Gentleman' and 'Old Dun Cow'.
Often hopping on the last bus home, compulsory chippy supper, followed by a spinning room as your head laid down attempting slumber.
Driving tests passed, rotating non-drinking driver, as couples, further venues sought for chicken in a basket with your brew.
Inns such as 'The Model T', the 'Beeswing', the 'Log Cabin', the 'Vintage', the 'Forresters Arms' and the *'Spotted Dog' all regularly visited.*

Such was the social culture of the 70s and 80s, that we participated in many a pub game,
From darts, pool, dominoes, cribbage, table football and even Pac-Man and space invaders.
Our other halves imbibing concoctions of Cinzano, Dubonnet, Martini, Snowball, Brandy and Babycham fame.
Keg beers squirted into handled, dimpled pint glasses, Watney's Red Barrel, Trophy Bitter, Double Maxim and

Double Diamond didn't work wonders.

*Drinking then stepped up a league as we entered the life
of an undergraduate with huge Uni bars galore.
Pub crawls, drinking games called boat races and fizz
buzz helped us unwind from our academic studies,
Or after our arduous college sports participation,
interspersed by an occasional party or dancing on the
disco floor.
Degrees in hand it was time to return home and enter the
world of work leaving the partying of beer behind
or was it?*

*Supplementing daytime income for our marriage and first
house, Carol worked in the Arden Arms serving
sumptuous beer.
Theakstons hand-pulled ales much appreciated by the
locals, family and of course myself.
Over the many years together we've worked hard and
played many sports without fear.*

Post games supping glorious cask ales like, Timothy Taylors Landlord, Hawkeshead Red, Tetleys and John Smith's Magnet were the attraction.

Then there were the special occasions of holidays, birthdays, weddings, farewells, christenings, new jobs etc., to be blessed
this time with tipples including red, white, rose wines, and champagne along with the likes of,
Grappa, Sambuca, Baileys, and port aperitifs as a coping mechanism for being stressed,
And genetically a social way of life from a Northeastern upbringing, masking the hard steps and choices in life.

Sat round a table with family, my son's friend called "My round, what you're all having?" I replied, "Bitter please, top half."
Dutifully to the bar he scuttled, returning with a tray of drinks and just a tiny half pint of bitter for me!
I cried, "How have you managed to fetch the top half, without the bottom?" To rapturous applause and many a larf.

Back to the bar, head down he went, returning with a glorious full pint. Such is the banter and socia life in a bar.

2017 for me, this sojourn and social experiment with alcohol ended with life-threatening epilepsy caused by a brain abscess.
The resulting choice was simple, no alcohol and therefore live, so far six years now teetotal.
Yet still as a top half, favourite beers supped, with names of Adnams Ghost Ship, Brew Dog Nanny State and Guiness.
Enjoying and celebrating life with a glass at least half full, being classed as zero percent.

Cheers!

26. Planche et Voile

Board hire at Shanklin on the idyllic Isle of Wight started the adventure,
In a wetsuit soon falling, and flipping like a sea lion from a white plank.
Yet somehow, I was already hooked to windsurfing that's for sure.
So it was back home to purchase all the equipment needed to undertake this thrilling sport.

Board, sail, boom, mast, life jacket and wetsuit dented my cash debenture.

Kit in tow it was off to the reservoir for RYA lessons and safety certification.
All in the centre of one of the UK's busiest road networks.
Who would have thought? Spaghetti junction!
Members of Tamworth windsurfing club we became, sailing with regularity,
on Borrow Pit Lake, fashioned from the ring road known as the Egg with affection.

In it for the long haul, or more precisely Uphaul, down haul and out haul.
All parts of the rig pulled, in order to trim the sail.
To perfect the angle of attack when the wind came to call.
Whether it be on a body of lake, sea or water.
Through all seasons the art was perfected, winter, spring summer or fall.

As windsurfers, we are all amateur meteorologists scouring weather applications, on our phone.
Watching for increasing winds, and ideal direction along with the tide's highs and lows.
We can be seen at the water's edge in deep discussion deciding the size of sail to hone.
Fingers in the air, or waving anemometers to check the wind speed in knots.
Looking for white horses riding the swirling, crashing crests, the Beaufort scale showing ready for fun.

At four and above with sail selected you beach start your board.
Planning above the maelstrom surface of water is your aim.
With the wind driving your face you hook into your boom surging forward.
Exhilaration of the challenge between your muscle sinews and the force of nature.
Always aware that at any point in time, from your board you may be catapulted.

*Throughout the country this passion pursued, from
Derwent, Semer and Rutland waters.
To Marazion, Cardigan, Beadnell and Morecambe bays
Bala, Coniston, Windermere, and Ullswater lakes.
On trailer, roof racks, and in caravans, the boards,
masts, sails and canoes stowed.
Even across the pond, this planche à voile continued on
French, Irish and Spanish shores.*

27. Volleyball

Following our wedding, our first home was in Ipswich, county town of sleepy Suffolk.
We entered the sports centre looking for a sport in which we could participate in unison.
A poster festooned on the wall simply said 'Ipswich Volleyball Club meets Fridays at 7 pm'.
So we attended our first meet in the gregarious pursuit of health, sport and social fun.

Starting with the volley, executed by a diamond shape between the fingers of both hands above your head.
Arms then extended to propel the soft ball in a high arc towards a teammate.
Next to master was the dig or low underhand pass performed by squatting,
With arms extended together out in front, the flat platform made as legs extend, the bump pass you create.

Two out of three ain't bad but now the spike or smash is next.
You approach the net, staring into space at its imposing 2.43 metres height.
Initiating a vertical jump, with swinging arms and smash contacting the ball above the net,
Powered with kinetic and potential energy down and out of sight.

With six players on court for each team, each side of the net, it is the ultimate team game.
Each team taking up to three consecutive touches to get the ball over the net such that the opponents are unable

to get it returned.

Although simple in concept, tactics abound as players must rotate positions both in attack and defence. Yet they can play in specialist positions by switching, once opponents have completed the ball being served.

From behind the baseline, the serve can be underhand, overhand firmly grounded or as a powerful, smashing jump.

Flying over the net, with opponents unable to connect, and onto their court floor it's deemed an Ace.

Play then continues, scoring points on your opponent's inability to return the ball,

until a team reaches a score of 25 points by at least a 2-point clear margin and a set won, being the case.

Generally, the best of five sets, wins the game for a team, though determined by league and competition rules. Thunderbirds and International Rescue have F.A.B. as a moniker; International Volleyball rules are sanctioned by the F.I.V.B.

Psychology and tactics support this skilful game as with

high fives each point won is celebrated by your team.
In position at the net, between opposing players banter is
riven as you express feigned sorrow at their errors made,
tee hee.

For 26 years I played this sport, in local, regional and
national leagues and competitions.
From East Anglia, East Midlands, West Midlands,
Durham, Northumberland to Teesside and Yorkshire.
Even on the beaches of Weston-Super-Mare, Bridlington,
Tynemouth and Corfu.
This playing career coming to an abrupt end, following a
diagnosis of a brain tumour.

Yet my love for this game did not diminish as for many
subsequent years continuing as a coach and referee.
Trying to bring the joy, thrills and skills of volleyball to a
new and wider audience.
Many, many friends have been made and retained
through its participation.
Hoping that this dig, volley and smash ditty stimulates
you to give it a go with some conscience.

28. En Guarde

Upon reaching sixth form, my focus drifted away from mainstream sport,
For many years as a fledgling, the cricket pitch was my field,
Yet this I abandoned as a lad from the comprehensive street
To join a fencing club, normally associated with the public-school elite.
Was it because bowlers were becoming faster and more perilous,
That I took up a sport which had an increased potential level of danger to yield!

The sports kit was also white with a box worn to protect your orchids.
Like a battle between bowler and batter in cricket,
You faced your adversary with a weapon of steel in a gloved hand,
And upon their torso, your target you hoped to find
As you lunged and darted along the 46-foot piste,
Instead of bounding along a strip called a 66-foot wicket.

Both sports were as gladiatorial as a game of chess.
Exhibiting skills of guile, disguise, attack and defence.
Another lexicon of language had to be recalled
Replacing gully, mid-wicket, silly mid-off, runs and no-balled,
With foil, epée, body cord, lamè, parry and riposte.
As Fleet footed you straight thrust your advance.

Watching swashbuckling Errol Flynn films brought me to the sport.
First attempt, foil in hand I fly-swatted away my opponent's sword,

Like a whirling pirate charging and clashing weapons on the gangplank.
It looked more like the Keystone Cops from films Top Rank.
After several practice sessions and moves demonstrated
Some skills unbelievably shone through observed.

Many hours wrist twirling of forte, foible and button of the blade ensued.
Until at last, competition bouts beckoned, and protective suit and helmets donned.
Plugged via a bungee cord to an electronic scoring box like a Christmas Tree.
Red light and green lights illuminating successful target hits for you and your opponent respectively.
A white light producing a gap in your adrenaline rush as you are both off target.
Frenetic, frantic, and frivolous three bouts of three minutes duelling until a winner found.

For over 30 years as a professional in the Pharmacy Arena, I presided over the dispensing of thousands and thousands of GP prescriptions. All are intended for the treatment of patients under our care.

The Pharmaceutical Industry has contributed massively to saving many lives and improving quality of life, and continues to do so. Yet sometimes, they veer from the path set out in their Research and Development innovations and good intentions, as drug use, over the years throws up unanticipated problems. This I have expressed in the following poem. 'Big Pharma'.

29. Big Pharma

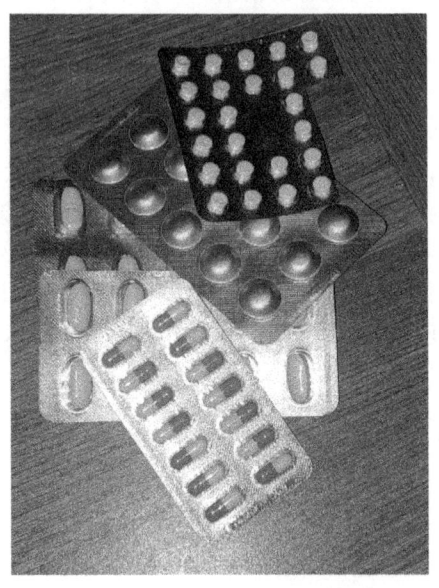

1940s: The miracle cure of penicillin hailed,
Yet resistance emerged where its promise had failed.

1950s: The mind was subdued with Chlorpromazine's sway,
But the cost was too great as health slipped away.

1960s: Thalidomide's shadow, a global disgrace,
Left children malformed, a stain hard to erase.

1970s: DES (Diethylstilboestrol), contraceptive hormones were touted with pride,
Yet cancers and loss were what they supplied.

1980s: Benzos for nerves, relief they'd bestow,
But addiction soon followed where trust used to grow.

1990s: Oxy's sweet lie brought pain to the land,
A nation enslaved by a corporate hand.

2000s: Stimulants pushed for distracted youth,
A generation entangled in half-hidden truths.

2010s and beyond: Fentanyl's reign and antidepressant despair,
Big Pharma grows richer, while lives disappear.

30. Pete

Forty years have passed since I met my good friend Pete,
With a similar warped sense of humour, straight away we gelled.
Sharing many an hour downing several quarts of Pedigree was regularly our feat,

Much to the despair of our wives yet also Ted the landlord of the Bird in Hand.
After such a session, a plan we did hatch
With, Treasurer John, Secretary Pete and Chairman Maurice, by the end of play
Austrey Amblers Cricket Club was formed from scratch,
And without a ground, all our matches had to be played away.

Pete would stride out to the crease armoured from head to toe,
With cricketing leg, thigh, and arm pads, topped with his trademark wide-brimmed hat.
He would make his mark, his eyes staring out the bowler who was making a fast run against his foe.
Pete in the style of Geoffrey Boycott would halt the swerving, bouncing ball with a deadpan bat.

Many a team we would frustrate, despite our losses mounting.
Yet one game, against Birmingham Municipal, stands out in folklore.

A win at last, we sunk pints and concoctions from the prized, duck-laden frying pan whilst singing and celebrating.
Having imbibed one too many, we had to be collected by Brenda and Carol.

A lasting memory, is laying an almost comatose Pete, amongst bats and pads onto the cricket equipment bag.
Then manhandling him to his awaiting Brenda, followed by an unceremonious dumping into their car.
With Pete and I in the team, two jokers in the pack, life was not a drag.
As we made our way home feeling elated; it was a good job our homes were not too far.

Pete would often be seen with bunches of keys in greater abundance than a Tower of London gaoler.
Many a pub and club he would attend in order to empty fag and gaming machines of their loot.
With bags and bags of coins, destined for the bank he would swagger,

To his beloved Volvo, depositing their abundant weight into its boot.

When his gaming license came up for renewal, I was asked to be a referee for his suitability.
Two police detective Sergeants rocked up at my door to check if he was a character of good repute and habit.
With many questions, a grilling they gave me, checking my own credibility.
Ensuring that, unlike his machines, Pete was not a one-armed bandit.

When we moved away from the Midlands we, regularly as good friends do, kept in contact,
Whether by e-mail or telephone, we shared jokes and anecdotes.
Over the years, to each other's homes would regularly visit,
Often for beers and of course for our favoured ruby murrays.

As a doting, devoted husband, father and grandfather,
Pete will be greatly missed, yet still much loved,
As he joined that great team in the sky, either cricketing or fishing with fly or feather.
Farewell, it has been a pleasure and honour my dear joker friend.

31. Marsh House Farm

From Marsh House Farm near Carnforth's way,
Morecambe Bay unfolds its grand expanse,
The morning mist begins to sway,
While sunlight casts its golden glance,
And distant shores in light's embrace dance.

The tide retreats, the sands laid bare,
Birds soar across the tranquil scene,
A painter's palette beyond compare,

Where water's edge meets meadows green,
And Warton Crag stands serene.

As noon ascends, the skies transform,
Clouds drift in patterns, slow and bright,
The craggy silhouette, weather-worn,
Holds secrets from the ancient night,
A sentinel in daylight's flight.

Afternoon's warm embrace does yield,
The bay, a mirror to the sky,
Ripples whisper tales concealed,
While farm fields bask in sun's soft sigh,
And shadows of the crag lie nigh.

Evening falls with hues of fire,
The horizon blushes in the west,
Reflections of the day retire,
To rest in Morecambe's gentle breast,
And Warton Crag in twilight dressed.

Night descends, the stars arise,
A celestial dance above the shore,
The moon's soft glow, a sweet surprise,
Illuminates the crag once more,
A beacon in the night's decor.

Dawn returns with gentle grace,
The bay awakens, fresh and new,
Warton Crag's enduring face,
Greets the day with a steadfast view,
From Marsh House Farm, a timeless cue.

32. Full Moon Rising

Above the hills, the sky is deep,
So lush, the night begins to sway,
An orange moon starts its silent creep,
When, reflecting off the bay,
It leaps, a golden path where waters lay.

The air is warm, a caressing breeze,
Pirouetting a soft ballet.
The moon's ascent puts minds at ease,
Its glow a spell, a quiet tease,
Enchanting Morecambe Bay.

The tides embrace to the moon's delight,
Waves whisper secrets, calm and slow,

Shadows dance in this tranquil night,
Their movements fluid, pure, and bright,
A soothing rhythm's gentle flow.

As night deepens, the stars appear,
Like a canopy of distant fires,
Yet the moon, stands sentinel, watching so near,
Its orange glow, both warm and clear,
Triggering endless dreams and desires.

33. Life on Hold

My plumbing has sprung a leak yet again.
Endlessly my brain tries a path to clear,
through the endless fog, drowsiness and pain.
Avoiding meningitis, still I live in fear,
All because of CSF rhinorrhoea,
Keeping life on hold

Imaging reveals many a hole,
All along the skull base,
Just like a colander bowl.
For neurosurgeons another case,

Major surgery for me to face
Whilst life on hold

Their belt and braces approach to anatomy
Incising across my skull, ear tip to ear tip
Then entering via a craniotomy,
To extensively plug and seal each gap,
With a pericranial flap.
Anaesthetist keeping my life on hold.

Despite a full day in the operating theatre,
With many a risk to endure.
It will be worthwhile to regain my character,
And once again to embrace the future
With a glass half-full, I'm sure.
No longer life on hold.

34. You look so well

Your neck is stiff and your head is pounding,
Your brain is lost in space and time
Low-pressure symptoms are continually clamping.
Nausea and brain fog constantly combine.
Yet you look so well.

Symptoms spiral out of control unabating.
With one pillow you lie horizontal for relief.
Yet with this solution's effect decreasing,
You try forty-five degrees with two pillows beneath
So you can look well.

Yet your ability to cope diminishes.
When will it be fixed?
Are your constant wishes
Your glass being emptied
But you look so well

The symptoms are all internal
No one can see
Your pain eternal
A great need for major surgery
So again, you can feel and look so well

35. Angel of Darlington

My angel first appeared to me across the classroom in the year 1971 AD
On earth innocuously as a smiley chattering vision, whence way back in 73,
By the chance of a dice throw at a party, a couple we were meant to be.

50 years later I am still together with
My Angel of Darlington.

Together so many memories and experiences unravelled.
Some so very sad and traumatic yet interspersed with
such happiness.
Of family life, work and friendships blessed
All in the partnership of a soulmate,
My Angel of Darlington

My angel wife appears in so many guises,
As, teacher, mother, grandma, aunt, friend, sister,
confidante, baker and nurse.
With so much unabated devoted care in equal measures.
For so many a lucky soul nestling under the caring
wings, of
My Angel of Darlington.

So much care and love is given despite wings which are
clipped,
By the battle scars of her immune system attacking its
own nervous system.

The resultant frailties of mobility and being constantly fatigued
do not inhibit the total care enveloped by Caggy,
My Angel of Darlington.

36. Bradford Lads

It was way back in '76
Whence freshers from all over Britain
Descended upon the Bradford University campus
There were Scottish, Welsh, as well as North, West, and East Yorkshiremen,
Including some Scousers, a Geordie and even a Mancunian

Into Revis Barber Halls of Residence
Studying for a divergent set of degrees,

Taking three to four years, facts and figures into furtive minds to condense
Topics including Pharmacy, Accountancy, Manufacturing systems Engineering, Peace Studies,
Also Human Purposes and communication, with grants paying their fees

Lifelong friendships being forged
With many a common activity including,
houses, parties, sports, and drinking being linked.
Alehouses with various titles, regularly visiting
The 'Shearbridge', 'Black Swan', 'Old House at Home',
'Jacobs Well' and 'The Peel' for serious supping.

Eating and dining cemented cultural experience development
With many a breakfast lunch and tea consumed in 'The Italia' and 'Candia' cafes
Weekend evening dining in 'Francos and Tonys' or 'La Luna' provided more refinement
Yet over time, our taste buds succumbed to many, many curries

*In the exotic establishments of 'The Shimla', 'The
Karachi', 'The Kashmir' and the 'The Taj' and 'Sheesh
Mahals',*

*Keeping fit and socialising encompassed football, rugby,
and rowing*
Basketball, Squash, Table football and Tennis
*Even participating in the dangerous and slippery pursuit
of Ice skating*
*Discotheques were frequently attended at Park Avenue
Cricket Club and Annabella's*
Though more of an excuse for imbibing after-hours

*We survived all this frivolity as well as some dubious
places of residence*
*Sometimes Adventuring into the JB Priestley library for
contemplation,*
Study, revision, photocopying, all with a stoic resilience
To facilitate our achievement and degree graduation
*Scrolls in hand Harold Wilson presided over the
presentation*

Between '79 and '80 we all left for gainful employment across the UK
Leaving behind National Front rallies and the winter of discontent,
Star Wars and Saturday Night Fever at the Odeon seemed far away
We vowed to keep in touch, which for 44 years we have managed with intent
Incorporating Reunions at least annually has been the arrangement

At venues countrywide including Liverpool, Oxford, Pembrokeshire,
The Lake District and of course Bradford to name but a few
Walking, conversing, reminiscing, and drinking like yesteryear
Topics such as politics, history and sport and other fat we'd chew
Likewise, sages or just grumpy old men, the changing world we view

As a WhatsApp group, we daily chat, sometimes as clowns
Continuing the support and banter for each other as we turn each page
Helping to cope with life's continuing ups and downs
Sharing wit, humour and imparting shared knowledge
As we continue our friendship long into old age

Simply the Bradford Lads

37. ONE to the power of twenty-ONE

ONE brain as two hemispheres acting as ONE master control unit

ONE vision of sight through two eyes

Two ears providing ONE sense of hearing

ONE mouth sounding out ONE voice

ONE nose with two nostrils infusing ONE sense of smell

Combining to provide ONE sense of taste

All housed in ONE skull

Two lungs to inhale ONE vital breath

ONE heart with four chambers functioning as ONE central pumping station

ONE digestive system providing essential nutrients and eliminating waste

ONE exoskeleton acting as a cage to protect all our functions parts

Aided by ONE skin to wrap us all up and feel the ONE sense of touch

All in all, ONE unique whole-body system

providing ONE life to live ONE love to give

And in its finality, ONE soul to set free

38. Foggy top

To repair my leaking colander of a skull base
The surgeon's vocabulary described it as a
"Bifrontal craniotomy and wide transcranial flap repair
of the anterior cranial fossa floor"
Simply, as the size of an open palm, the skull was drilled
to produce the trap door
As a passageway, exposing my neuro centre, my brain
Under which an incised layer of scalp took pride of place

For many days and nights, I languished on the hospital ward

Experiencing pain, nausea and a drug-induced zombie-like state
Vaguely aware of my surroundings, people, events and lacking true cognition
Until all tubes and stitches were removed and improvements made in my condition
Then the Occupational Therapist was summoned to observe
Tea and toast making before, to take me home Carol was called

At home, the body began to repair and heal, yet the brain wanted to remain in stasis
Every day, as hours ticked by, my brain switched off from all stimuli
Sleep curls its tendrils around, beckoning me to doze and nap
With mist descending a foggy mountaintop
At most times I know who I am, but is it me?
More testing and support required by the Neuro-rehabilitation service

Three months have passed since that trap door opened
It was time for a review, headaches rescinding yet again my nose began to drip
Another CSF leak is suspected together with a VP shunt blockage and malfunction
More CT and MRI scans to light me up like a Christmas tree decoration
More operations beckon such that through the fog
I feel, that I'm in a maze back to where it all started

39. Cyborg, Titanium Man

From flesh to alloy, a tale to unfold,
A cyborg forged with titanium bold.
Bone-anchored hearing aid whispers guide me through,
With grace sounds from the outside world vibrating new.

A VP (ventriculoperitoneal) shunt does flow,
Through my body rivers of CSF in rhythmic glow.
With a shunt assistant anti-syphon guardian,
ever so wise,
Balancing tides, where over or under pressure lies.

An Orbis Sigma II pressure valve keeps vigil inside,
Measuring thoughts where my mind does reside.
Its silent watch ensures the calm,
A mechanical hymn, a soothing psalm.

Three small plates, a craniotomy's seal,
Screws hold steadfast where wounds did heal.
Temporal bone flaps no longer fight,
Titanium shields gleam in the light.

An artificial hip, a pivot of might,
Moves with grace, day and night.
Joints reborn, a second chance,
A metallic rhythm, life's new dance.

This body, rebuilt, a marvel to see,
Where human and machine entwine so free.
The sum of its parts, a paradox grand,
Strength in the metal, soul in the hand.

Cyborg, I stand, with purpose aglow,
Bearing the scars, the paths I know.
Titanium warrior, steadfast and true,

I am myself, a being anew.
Perhaps my body has already been donated to the NHS
For the wonders of neuro-surgical endeavours
When I depart this land so pleasant and free
As Titanium Man please recycle me

40. BEDLAM

Yet again, in hospital I am bound
Brain under attack from its own defences
It can, one minute be bursting at the seams
Or next vacuumed as fluid seeps away dreams
All in balance and stasis the body compenses

In silence sought but never found,
Machines beep endlessly through the night,
A restless cacophonous pulse that stirs the air,

As shadows drift in unmuted care,
And dreams dissolve in sterile light.

A weary heart, a mind unbound,
Awake as noisy footsteps weave and wane,
Monitors hum their ceaseless song,
The days are blurred, the nights too long,
Awaiting answers wrapped in pain.

Ocean blue and clear curtained spaces barely hold,
A fragile hope, a whispered fear,
Conversations, not so hushed but clear,
Echo thoughts I dread to hear,
As bodies mend or break, untold.

The clock ticks slow, its face too bold,
While voices rise in distant strain,
Sleep, elusive, slips away,
Yet time insists it will not stay,
Caught between the still and strain.

Through twilight's veil, the ward unfolds,
With sterile sheets and quiet dread,
The tests approach, a shadowed fate,
Decisions balanced, evermore risks await,
Surgery looms once again, above the bed.

But dawn may bring a peace foretold,
A healing light to pierce the haze,
Through every beep, each whispered sigh,
A glimmer grows within the eye,
And hope sustains the longest days

Thanks to the love of family and friends around us
We can endeavour passaging our neuro-diversity
Keeping a glass half full with young thoughts of fun
Fighting together many a battle against Adversity
As time fleetingly passes, away from bedlam we begin to run

41. Bloodsucker

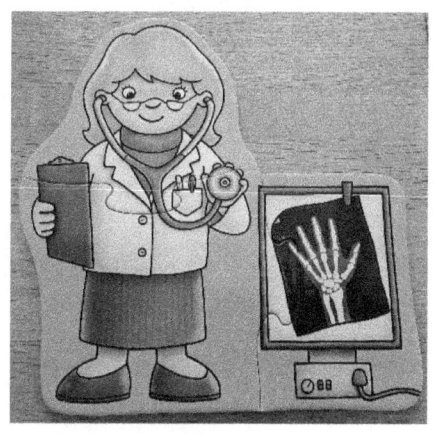

I was dreaming of a far eastern sandy beach
When suddenly there was a blast of light above my head
Shimmering in the afterglow, just out of reach,
Shrouded in mask and gown at the end of my bed,
With remote control in hand raising it up,
as if from the dead

The phlebotomist utters the immortal words,
No wonder nicknamed the vampire nurse
"I've come to take your bloods"
Also "Sharp scratch" or "prick" hissed as in a curse.
Wherein, the blinding light makes my headache worse

Then as in shadowed halls where silence grows,
A needle's whisper finds its mark.
Soft hands, like ghosts, in practised flows,
Draw crimson streams within the light and dark,
A quiet dance, precise and stark.

The room hums low, a measured beat,
Faint footsteps echo on the tile.
Through tangled dreams and sheets, they meet—
A fleeting touch, a fleeting trial,
Gone swiftly with a whispered smile.

In slumber's grip, the world feels thin,
Where bloodlines trace the unseen thread.
They come and go with quiet spin,
In secret rites beside your bed,
Till morning breaks, and they have fled

Whisking away four vials of my burgundy essence,
To their lair for testing and experimentation
Measuring U&E levels for sodium, potassium and magnesium presence

Checking liver and kidney function
Also as vampires do, a full blood count is their intention

The stars fade faint beyond the pane,
As dawn prepares its muted climb.
A fleeting pinch, a fading strain,
Time ticks along in steady rhyme,
The night's last act, in measured time.

42. Cisternogram

Beneath the cold, unyielding light,
I lie and wait for science's gaze,
The needles prick, the dye takes flight,
Through whispered veins in shadowed haze.
A silent stream, it charts its way,
To maps unseen in dread's ballet.

The hum of machines fills the air,
A sombre tune to match my fear.
Technicians move with practised care,
Their faces calm, my thoughts unclear.

What secrets will their glances glean,
In the glow of a phosphorescent scene?

Time falters in this sterile tomb,
Its passage stretched and thin as air.
The walls close in, a shadowed womb,
A cradle for my growing despair.
I count the tiles, their cracks and lines,
Seeking solace in imagined signs.

The whispers start—the questions, fears,
What will they find, what lies within?
The dark unknown tugs at my tears,
A quiet war I cannot win.
The dye, it dances, slowly sways,
A spectre weaving through the maze.

The waiting room, a purgatory,
Where hope and dread take turns to reign.
Each step they take feels accusatory,
Each rustling paper a whispered pain.
I glance at doors, at fleeting eyes,

A battlefield where courage dies.

What if the map shows faults and flaws,
A breach, a break, a place gone wrong?
Will surgeons come with sterile claws,
Or healing hands with purpose strong?
I fear the answer, fear the choice,
A future held in a stranger's voice.

And when the words at last do fall,
A verdict sealed in sterile prose,
The world will tilt, the shadows call,
The path ahead in starkness glows.
But through the dark, I'll chart my way,
A fragile hope for brighter days.

43. The Song of the CT Scanner

Well here I am again across 17 years,
Having had well in excess of a ton of CT scans
An X-Ray tube, in a doughnut-shaped machine, rotating
focused beam of X rays emitting

Chorus:
Clang, clang, a hammer's song,
A piercing cry that won't belong.
Whirr and click, the rhythm spins,
The symphony of scanning begins.

Inside the tube, I lay, on a motorised table, still and tight,
Moving as a cocoon of steel in the sterile white.
Into its mouth as the walls curve close, a mechanical embrace,
Each hum and buzz fills the echoing space.

Chorus:
Clang, clang, a hammer's song,
A piercing cry that won't belong.
Whirr and click, the rhythm spins,
The symphony of scanning begins.

Detectors measuring the intensity of the rays passing through my body
bone, muscle, fat absorb X-rays each to a varying degree,
creating a pattern of attenuation,
a detailed 3D representational image in cross-section

Chorus:
Clang, clang, a hammer's song,
A piercing cry that won't belong.
Whirr and click, the rhythm spins,

The symphony of scanning begins.

Upon a monitor images, adjusted for contrast and
brightness are displayed
forming specific views for analysis for medic's aid,
with variations in tissue density supporting diagnoses
For conditions such as tumours, fractures, or vascular
diseases.

Chorus:
Clang, clang, a hammer's song,
A piercing cry that won't belong.
Whirr and click, the rhythm spins,
The symphony of scanning begins.

My brain is imaged for chamber(ventricle) abnormality,
VP shunt position and functionality,
For holes and fissures within my skull
Contributing to pressure change, leaks and CSF levels
half-full

Chorus:

Clang, clang, a hammer's song,
A piercing cry that won't belong.
Whirr and click, the rhythm spins,
The symphony of scanning begins.

A voice from nowhere whispers "Don't move"
As magnets spin with a precise groove.
My heartbeat blends with the roaring sound,
A strange new melody profound.

Chorus:

Clang, clang, a hammer's song,
A piercing cry that won't belong.
Whirr and click, the rhythm spins,
The symphony of scanning begins.

Eyes shut tight, I drift to a plane,
Of thoughts that mirror the scan of my brain.
The noise becomes waves that carry me far,
Beyond the room, where dreams bizarre.

Chorus:

Clang, clang, a hammer's song,
A piercing cry that won't belong.
Whirr and click, the rhythm spins,
The symphony of scanning begins.

And when it's done, the world returns,
The silence hums: for results my body yearns.
Also, the weight of life outside the dome,
From the scanner's song, I venture home

44. Hospital Helping Hands

In Salford's ward, where stillness hums,
We gather stories, day and night.
Our scars, like maps, show where fate comes,
Through pain and change, the future drums,
A bond of strength through shared insight.

We rise, we fall, we share our plight,
Through fractured days and endless night.
From different worlds, one path we see,
In healing's hands, we're set to be.
A barrister, once sharp and keen,

Who fought for justice, right or wrong,
Now speaks of trials he's ever seen,
His wit intact, her spirit serene,
His voice, though tired, remains so strong.

We rise, we fall, we share our plight,
Through fractured days and endless night.
From different worlds, one path we see,
In healing's hands, we're set to be.

The engineer recalls his line,
Where cups were formed for countless pills.
His spine, now stitched, begins to align,
He dreams of work, of purpose divine,
His hope rebuilt through surgeon's skills.

We rise, we fall, we share our plight,
Through fractured days and endless night.
From different worlds, one path we see,
In healing's hands, we're set to be.

A taxi driver, life askew,
His wheels and world once spun so fast.
He speaks of fares and streets he knew,
Now anchored here, his strength renew,
He looks ahead, unbound at last.

We rise, we fall, we share our plight,
Through fractured days and endless night.
From different worlds, one path we see,
In healing's hands, we're set to be.

A teacher dreams of lessons taught,
Her pupils' faces bright and near.
Her battle won, though dearly bought,
Her passion burns, her mind has caught
A future where her course is clear.

We rise, we fall, we share our plight,
Through fractured days and endless night.
From different worlds, one path we see,
In healing's hands, we're set to be.

By day, we share a silent will,
By night, our voices echo wide.
Through scars and tales, we find a thrill,
For life, though shaken, lingers still,
And hope becomes our constant guide.

We rise, we fall, we share our plight,
Through fractured days and endless night.
From different worlds, one path we see,
In healing's hands, we're set to be.

45. The resonant MRI

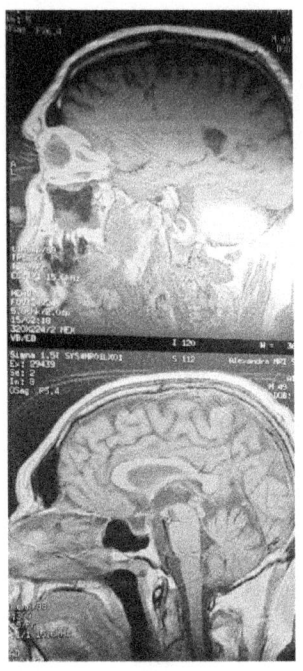

Lying still, in a tunnel tight, the cold machine begins to hum,
Superconducting magnets cooled by liquid helium,
strong magnetic fields tuned to the resonant frequency of hydrogen atoms
resulting in absorbing energy, misaligning many protons.
Whirr, whirr, thud, thud, the metal roars,
Click, clack, the radio frequency pulse pours,

then stops, the protons relaxing, releasing energy signals
detected in the scanner by a multitude of coils

Pulse, pulse, THRUM, THRUM, THRUM, a steady hum,
Clink, clank, BEAT, BEAT, BEAT a rising drum.
Buzz, Buzz, BLAST, BLAST, BLAST the rhythm shifts,
Echoes deep in twisting rifts.

Gradient magnets varying the magnetic fields
To precisely identify hydrogen atom locations
Computers processing, creating images for all to see
Ensuring the building of a map in 3D
Steady pulse, then silence falls,
In the machine, the darkness calls.
Whirring whispers, echoes deep,
Like thunder stirring from my sleep.

Pulse, pulse, THRUM, THRUM, THRUM, a steady hum,
Clink, clank, BEAT, BEAT, BEAT a rising drum.
Buzz, Buzz, BLAST, BLAST, BLAST the rhythm shifts,
Echoes deep in twisting rifts.

The world outside, a distant place,
Unknowingly unsure of my fate to face,
I'm wrapped in silence, floating still,
Captured by the scanners will
The lights above flicker, then fade,
The moments stretch, a quiet raid.
Inside, my skull boxed tight inside a frame,
An image born, whatever its future, whatever its name

Pulse, pulse, THRUM, THRUM, THRUM, a steady hum,
Clink, clank, BEAT, BEAT, BEAT a rising drum.
Buzz, Buzz, BLAST, BLAST, BLAST the rhythm shifts,
Echoes deep in twisting rifts.

The noise grows louder, sharp and clear,
A distant rhythm, not yet near.
I hold my breath, my thoughts grow thin,
The world outside has lost its spin.
And in this place, I cannot roam,
A silent witness, far from home.
But soon the hum will ebb away,
And I'll return to light of day.

46. A Christmas for Carol and I

The clock struck twelve, and all was not well,
In our chamber, where restless shadows dwell.
Beside me there lay, in a stormy oasis
My love, whose slumber rattled by progressive multiple sclerosis

First, a whistle, faint, then a groan so deep,
A steam train roused from the depths of sleep.

The engine hummed, a rhythmic refrain,
Crescendoing fast like a speeding train.

Clickety-clack, the carriages clashed,
Their thunderous cadence cruelly smashed
The fragile hopes of rest's soft hand,
As I lay awake in a sleepless land.

And lo! The spasms, those dreadful spasms,
Limbs flailing wild in terrible chasms!
A leg shot out with a thumping pound,
An arm careened in an arc profound.

"Oh mercy!" I cried, "What tempest is this,
That swirls all around stealing my bliss?
Will sleep's sweet touch ne'er grace my eyes?
Must I bear till dawn these nocturnal cries?"

The train grew fierce; its wheels did scream,
A cacophony-born disturbance, is it a dream?
The couplings clanged, the pistons roared,
And my poor love's muscles kicked and soared.

Yet as the night stretched, long and lean,
A thought arose: Could there be unseen
A magic stirring in this chaos wild—
The spirit of Christmas, tender and mild?

For amidst the racket and troubled night,
I spied, in my head a vision of light,
Father Christmas, a twinkle in his eye,
Paused by our chimney as the train steamed by.

"Patience, dear soul," he whispered low,
"For love endures, though the night may sow
Discord, and dreams seem far from near,
The morning shall dawn, bright and clear."

So I lay back down, amidst snoring steam and thrash,
The thunderous rhythm, the flail and crash,
And prayed for sleep to act as chief,
A Christmas balm, a welcome relief.

Thus, though the night was a stormy affair,
Love kept its watch in the midnight air.

For even through trials, our hearts hold fast,
To the peace of Christmas, come at last.

47. Sweet Dreams For Christmas

The firelight flickers, the stockings are hung,
Grandchildren dream of the gifts they'll find.
Their letters to Santa, written with care,
Of dolls and prams, games to share,
Hope glowing bright in their young, eager mind.

A three-year-old's wish is sweet and pure,
Twin dolls in a pram, side by side.

Fern pictures them, pink and blue swaddled in an embrace,
Imagines their smiles, their gentle grace,
And the joy of being their maternal guide.

Her six-year-old brother Oliver can barely sit still,
Table football and games he craves.
He dreams of goals in a thrilling match,
Of hockey and ping-pong, a perfect catch,
Playing Snooker in a world where balls drop in waves.

The letters were posted in a bright red box,
With wishes tucked in a glowing flame.
Each word held magic, a silent plea,
To wake and find gifts beneath the tree,
Bearing the signs of Santa's name.

The house is hushed, and the clock ticks slow,
Two little hearts thrum with delight.
They whisper of elves and a jingling sleigh,
Of reindeer flying far away,
Bringing treasures through the starlit night.

At dawn, they'll run to the sparkling tree,
Where dreams take shape in a festive array.
Twin dolls will wait in a pram so fine,
Games of skill on a table divine,
And laughter will crown their Christmas Day.

48. The 12 Days of Motown Christmas

On the first day of Christmas, my true love gave to me,
A record from the Supremes in harmony!

On the second day of Christmas, my true love gave to me,
Two Marvin Gayes,
And a record from the Supremes in harmony!

On the third day of Christmas, my true love gave to me,
The Three Degrees,
Two Marvin Gayes,
And a record from the Supremes in harmony!

On the fourth day of Christmas, my true love gave to me,
Four Tops a-swaying,
The Three Degrees,
Two Marvin Gayes,
And a record from the Supremes in harmony!

On the fifth day of Christmas, my true love gave to me,
Five Golden Tempts!
Four Tops a-swaying,
The Three Degrees,
Two Marvin Gayes,
And a record from the Supremes in harmony!

On the sixth day of Christmas, my true love gave to me,
Six Smokey lyrics,
Five Golden Tempts!
Four Tops a-swaying,
The Three Degrees,
Two Marvin Gayes,
And a record from the Supremes in harmony!

On the seventh day of Christmas, my true love gave to me,
Seven Vandellas dancing,
Six Smokey lyrics,
Five Golden Tempts!
Four Tops a-swaying,
The Three Degrees,
Two Marvin Gayes,
And a record from the Supremes in harmony!

On the eighth day of Christmas, my true love gave to me,
Eight Gladys Pips,
Seven Vandellas dancing,
Six Smokey lyrics,
Five Golden Tempts!
Four Tops a-swaying,
The Three Degrees,
Two Marvin Gayes,
And a record from the Supremes in harmony!

On the ninth day of Christmas, my true love gave to me,
Nine Miracles grooving,

Eight Gladys Pips,
Seven Vandellas dancing,
Six Smokey lyrics,
Five Golden Tempts!
Four Tops a-swaying,
The Three Degrees,
Two Marvin Gayes,
And a record from the Supremes in harmony!

On the tenth day of Christmas, my true love gave to me,
Ten Jacksons moonwalking,
Nine Miracles grooving,
Eight Gladys Pips,
Seven Vandellas dancing,
Six Smokey lyrics,
Five Golden Tempts!
Four Tops a-swaying,
The Three Degrees,
Two Marvin Gayes,
And a record from the Supremes in harmony!

On the eleventh day of Christmas, my true love gave to me,
Eleven Stevie wonders,
Ten Jacksons moonwalking,
Nine Miracles grooving,
Eight Gladys Pips,
Seven Vandellas dancing,
Six Smokey lyrics,
Five Golden Tempts!
Four Tops a-swaying,
The Three Degrees,
Two Marvin Gayes,
And a record from the Supremes in harmony!

On the twelfth day of Christmas, my true love gave to me,
Twelve Diana winks,
Eleven Stevie wonders,
Ten Jacksons moonwalking,
Nine Miracles grooving,
Eight Gladys Pips,
Seven Vandellas dancing,
Six Smokey lyrics,

Five Golden Tempts!
Four Tops a-swaying,
The Three Degrees,
Two Marvin Gayes,
And a record from the Supremes in harmony!

49. Carol's 67-year timeline

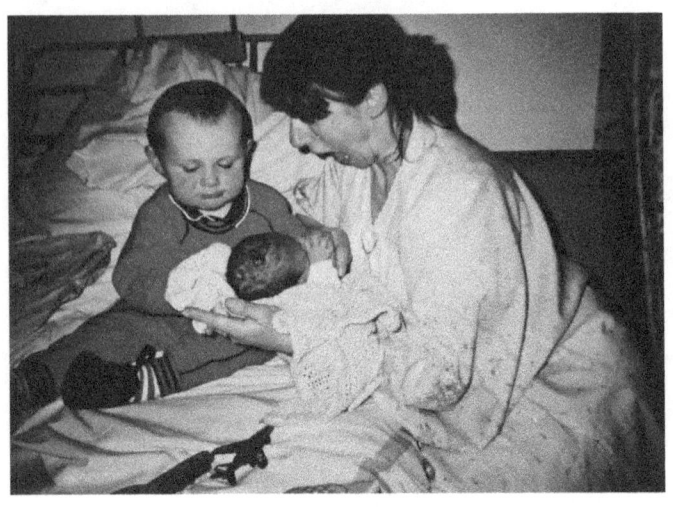

1958, Carol Ann Brookes arrived, a new light to shine,
1959, Castro claimed Cuba, a revolutionary sign.
1960, the laser beamed its first dazzling ray,
1961, Yuri Gagarin soared beyond Earth's clouds so grey.

1962, the Cuban Missile Crisis brought fear near,
1963, Dr. King spoke of dreams loud and clear.
1964, the Beatles took America by storm,
1965, civil rights began to take reform.

1966, England triumphed in the World Cup's embrace,
1967, South Africa's first heart transplant won the race.
1968, Martin and Bobby both tragically fell,
1969, Apollo 11—the Moon knew humanity well.

1970, the Beatles dissolved, a legend's end,
1971, microprocessors started to ascend.
1972, the Watergate scandal began its course,
1973, Carol and John became an item, Skylab launched, a new space force.

1974, Nixon resigned amidst scandalous despair,
1975, the Vietnam War ended, its burden laid bare.
1976, Hull College attended as Concorde sliced through skies, fast and keen,
1977, Elvis left the stage, a loss unforeseen.

1978, Louise Brown, the first test-tube baby, arrived,
1979, Bachelor of Education attained, as Margaret Thatcher's reign politically thrived.
1980, Mount St. Helens unleashed a fiery cascade,

1981, 11th July Carol and John Atkinson's union was made.
1982, the Falklands War shook islands far away,
1983, the internet's foundation began to lay.
1984, India wept as Indira Gandhi was slain,
1985, Live Aid united the world through music's refrain.

1986, Chernobyl burned with devastating heat,
1987, the stock market crash hit Wall Street.
1988, 10th September Our son Lewis born under blue, blue skies,
1989, the Berlin Wall crumbled before our eyes.

1990, April 11, Our son Sean was born with a cry,
1991, the Cold War ended, no longer awry.
1992, Bosnia was torn by a brutal war, for sure
1993, Our son Ross was lost—a heartache to endure.

1994, Mandela rose as apartheid's foe fell,
1995, the Oklahoma bombing—a tale to tell.
1996, Dolly the sheep was cloned, science to amaze,
1997, Diana left, the world in a daze.

1998, Google began its quest for knowledge to share,
1999, the Y2K bug gave the world a scare.
2000, the new millennium brought hope in sight,
2001, the Twin Towers fell, a haunting night.

2002, the Euro unified nations anew,
2003, Saddam fell, a dictator subdued.
2004, tsunamis struck Asia with a mighty roar,
2005, Hurricane Katrina devastated the shore.

2006, with an Adriatic cruise we celebrated our Silver Wedding Anniversary,
2007, John's Epidermoid emerged, and the iPhone launched, hi-lighting such advanced technology.
2008, Obama rose as history's first Black U.S. president,
2009, Michael Jackson's passing, a pop culture lament.

2010, Haiti quaked and cried in despair,
2011, Osama bin Laden's reign ended with a stare.
2012, Curiosity roved on Mars' sandy plains, its secrets to unfold.

2013, Carol's Multiple Sclerosis diagnosis rocked our world.
2014, Ebola's shadow darkened the lands,
2015, Paris mourned from terror's hands.
2016, the UK chose to break from the EU,
2017, #MeToo echoed truths long overdue.

2018, 22nd April, grandson Oliver was born, bringing cheer,
2019, Notre Dame burned, its spire disappeared.
2020, Covid, a pandemic reshaped the world we knew,
2021, 16th March, granddaughter Fern joined us, a life so bright and new.

2022, the James Webb telescope gazed into the past,
2023, artificial intelligence advanced so fast.
2024, Carol at clickety-click, a matriarch so wise,
2025 at 67 years her journey continues under life's vast skies.

50. Apoth Acky's Journey Through History

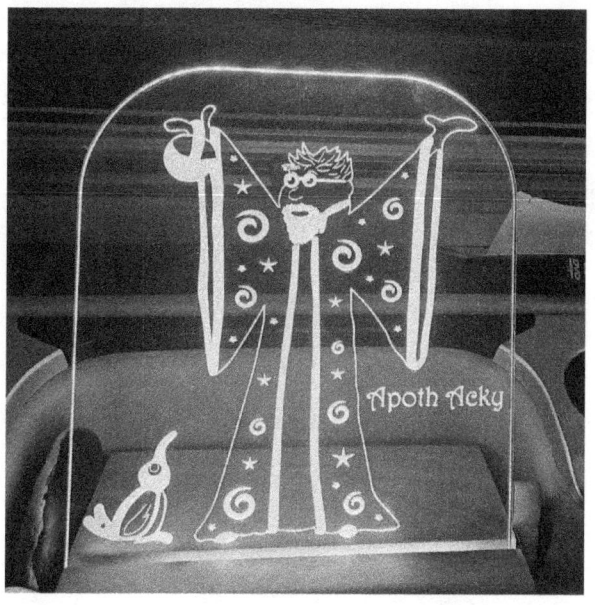

At Per Ankh, in Egypt's sands, where the Nile winds flow,
The 'Pepperers' and 'Spicers' learnt their skilful art,
Concocting and mixing their potions and lotions
so bright,
Peppered remedies would start to grow,
A healing touch that played its part,
Binding wounds in the moon's soft glow.

In Roman halls, with marble gleam,
The 'Pharmakopoles' learned their trade,
Crafting potions of fragrant might,
Mixtures danced in their herbal dream,
Mortars and pestles, measures and jars conveyed,
Potions for healing wars under stars pale light.

Beneath the stars, in cloisters still,
Alchemists dreamed of gold's delight,
Seeking elixirs for life's decay,
From roots and herbs, they plied their skill,
Charting realms of day and night,
Through veils of smoke, their wisdom lay.

Through darkened times, the plague's cruel breath,
Brought whispers of curative lore,
Apothecaries guarded their rites,
Peppered tinctures fought looming death,
In shadowed shops, their skill would soar
Illuminating the blackened nights.

The Middle Ages brought grim despair,
Plagues swept lands with deadly flight,
Chemists sought cures with fervent zeal,
From peppers ground, a healing prayer,
Potions brewed in candlelight,
A bitter salve for wounds to heal.

In castles high and in village square,
The Company of Grocers toiled, controlling and feared,
Such that Apothecaries, with mortar and pestle,
shaped the fight,
Powders and flames floated in the air.
Reading formulae from where secrets abide,
Balancing nature's dark and light

The Victorian age, with gaslight's glow,
Saw chemists and druggists rise with newfound art,
A world of science began to ignite,
Crushing and mixing still had its show,
In nature's lab, they played their part,
Uniting craft with industrial might.

Edwardian charm, a genteel grace,
Witnessed the chemist's growing fame,
Complex formulas filled the air,
Druggists lingered in their old place,
Their delicate skills remaining the same,
Binding past to progress rare.

In Edwardian shops, where oils were poured,
Shelves lined high with herbs and cream,
Pharmacists worked with learned care,
Secretly concocting potions, their craft adored,
A symbol tied to science's dream,
Of such pure knowledge, rich and rare.

In the bustling streets of years long gone,
Druggists crafted tinctures keen,
From peppercorns to fragrant blooms,
Each bottle marked with labels drawn,
Their potions healed, their powders clean,
Magicking cures for shadowed rooms

The Apothecary gave way to the lab,
And the chemist transformed into the druggist's trade,
Modern blends of precision and flair,
Still poisons in fluted bottles would grab,
Binding time's threads in healing's cascade,
An ancient echo in sterile care.

From humble roots to towering spires,
Pharmacists emerged with learned skill,
Combining history with modern might,
The twentieth century roared with coal fires.
As Pharmacists donned pristine white clinical gown,
A timeless art in the modern fight.

The 21st century bears its might,
With Chemists forging stronger ground,
Pharmacists bloomed with modern flair,
Technicians observed in dispensary's dim light,
The pharmacist's role has found new ground,
Gene Therapy, a future bound, with hope and care.

In labs today, where robots hum,
Where breakthroughs vast and cures are found
Crafting cures with precision's light,
Remind us all as to where we come from.
The worldwide web, a link profound,
Connecting the past with science's height.

EPILOGUE

I don't know what the future holds for us, and future generations, yet share with you a short poem starting with our "Boomer" generation.

Our Modern Generations

Twixt Perry Como's 'Prisoner of love', 1946 and The Beatles 'Can't Buy Me Love',1964
Boomers were born to the echoes of post-war relief,
Built their lives on the rubble of grief.
Dreams of prosperity and a painted boundary fence,
Yet Cold War shadows made progress tense.
Climate debates they didn't foresee,
A legacy of growth, but at what cost to air, land and sea?

From between The Who debuting 'My Generation', 1965 and The Police 'Don't Stand So Close To Me' 1980,
Born as latchkey kids, Generation X raised in a changing tide,
Divorce and recessions shaped their stride.
Tech pioneers in a pre-digital age,

Balancing tradition with innovation's stage.
A quiet resilience, overlooked by many,
Now facing midlife with pockets half-empty.

Born between Soft Cell's 'Tainted Love' in 1981 to the
Fugees' 'Killing Me Softly', 1996,
In a world of increasing speed,
Millennials were promised the stars, burdened with need.
Global recessions and towering debt,
Dreams deferred, but they haven't quit just yet.
Social media's glare, both boon and bane,
Seeking purpose in a world of pain.

As Elton John's Dianna tribute 'Candle in the Wind'
blew in 1997 to Carly Rae Jepson's 'Call Me Maybe'
2012,
In came Gen Z, the digital natives, born into screens,
Voices loud, challenging old regimes.
Mental health struggles they wear on their sleeve,
Questioning truths others might believe.
Climate warriors, with time running out,
A generation of hope, but racked with doubt.

Then, as Robin Thicke's 'Blurred Lines,' in 2013 through to 2024 and Sabrina Carpenter's 'Espresso'.
Generation Alpha appeared, toddlers of tech, with AI by their side,
In a world reshaped, where boundaries collide.
A future of jobs yet to be known,
Navigating spaces where none have grown.
Will they lead with wisdom, or falter with ease?
The burden of tomorrow rests on these.

Unborn yet, or as at 2025 Generation Beta, are only just here,
Theirs is a world we only fear.
Robots and algorithms chart their way,
A planet's health hangs on their sway.
Will they find peace in a fractured land,
Or build new worlds with a steady hand?

Shared Challenges lie in the distant past and futures, as
Each generation, a link in the chain,
Bearing burdens of progress and pain.
Lessons unlearned, or passed down too late,

Struggling to rewrite the course of fate.
Together they rise, divided they fall,
The weight of history binds them all.

Back to the present day and bringing my story back up to date, (as of January 2025), I have had my latest neurosurgical operation, changing the anti-siphon device in my neck as part of my VP shunt revision. As I was recovering, and having seen the operation suture clips in my neck, my brain signals coalesced into the thoughts for a poem, this time entitled 'Kurgan'.

This was stimulated by memories from one of my favourite films, 'Highlander'.

The Kurgan was a fictional character, in said film, an immortal and main antagonist to Connor Macleod the Highlander. He is portrayed as a rock punk-Frankenstein-type character, with a stitched-on head, punctuated by safety pins.

I also visualised his head being chopped off by Connor Macleod and beams of energy emanating from the wound. This vision was supplemented by the Queen song 'Don't Lose Your Head' from their album 'A Kind of Magic', from which accompanied several soundtracks for the film.

'Don't Lose Your Head' was composed by Taylor and features Joan Armatrading in cameo. The song takes its name from a line spoken in Highlander and is played for a short time when Kurgan kidnaps Brenda. The song then segues into a cover of 'Theme from New York, New York', though it is only a small clip.

My poem:-

Kurgan

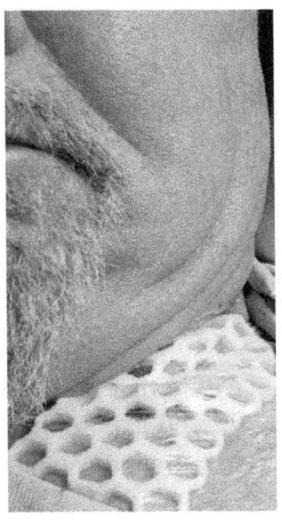

Beneath the sterile glow of the surgical light,
Two hours vanished into the folds of night.
A silent team worked steady, keen and deft,
To replace the guardian deep in my neck's cleft.
The hum of machines marked life's fragile fight.

Under the veil of anaesthetic's embrace,
Dreams were suspended in a timeless space.
A shunt reborn with its Miethke anti-syphon guide,
An intricate fix where technology abides,
Leaving its story etched upon my face.

Awakening, in recovery, to the sting of clips that bind,
A line of metal, my neck redesigned.
The wound like a zip, precise and grim,
I felt a kinship with The Kurgan's hymn,
A warrior marked by scars entwined.

The days that followed carried healing's ache,
Each twinge a proof of the strength we make.
Skin knits together as stitches fall away,
Yet the memory of the blade will always stay,
A badge of battles fought for life's sake.

Now I walk, hopefully, a little stronger each day,
A shunt secure, the price I'll gladly pay.
The mirror reflects a warrior's grin,
For scars are not the end, but where we begin
Proof that even in pain, life finds its way.

So all that is left for me to say is, 'Habenda Ratio Valetudinis' (Take account of health):

With every breath, a sacred trust,
Account for health—a duty just.
"Habenda Ratio Valetudinis," we say,
To guard life's gift, come what may.

Through mindful acts and wisdom's art,
We heal the body, mend the heart.
For health must shine, both near and far,
Our guiding light, our Northern Star.

Acknowledgements

You are all so special.
Carol, and our family (both immediate and extended).

My friends who, without you all.
My glass would be empty and cracked.

A big thank you is my call.
For being there as needed.

To all my readers and reviewers.
Following my life story all along the way.

For all those no longer physically near
Yet, to us, so, so, so dear

Blossom Spring my publishers.
For keeping it alive day by day.

www.blossomspringpubishing

www.ingramcontent.com/pod-product-compliance
Lightning Source LLC
Chambersburg PA
CBHW022358040426
42450CB00005B/242